How to Draw
BUGS

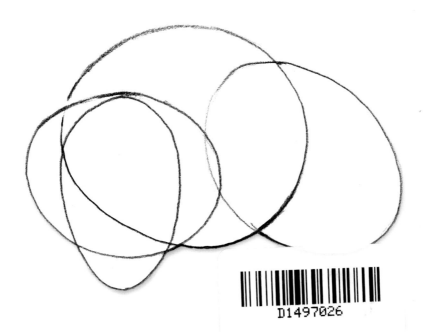

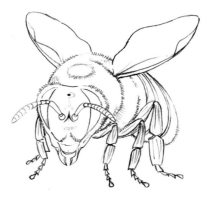

How to Draw
BUGS

Author
Lisa Regan

Artist
Steve Roberts

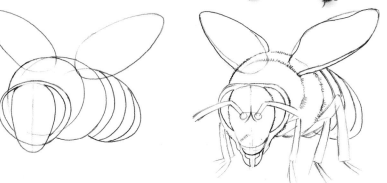

Miles
Kelly

contents

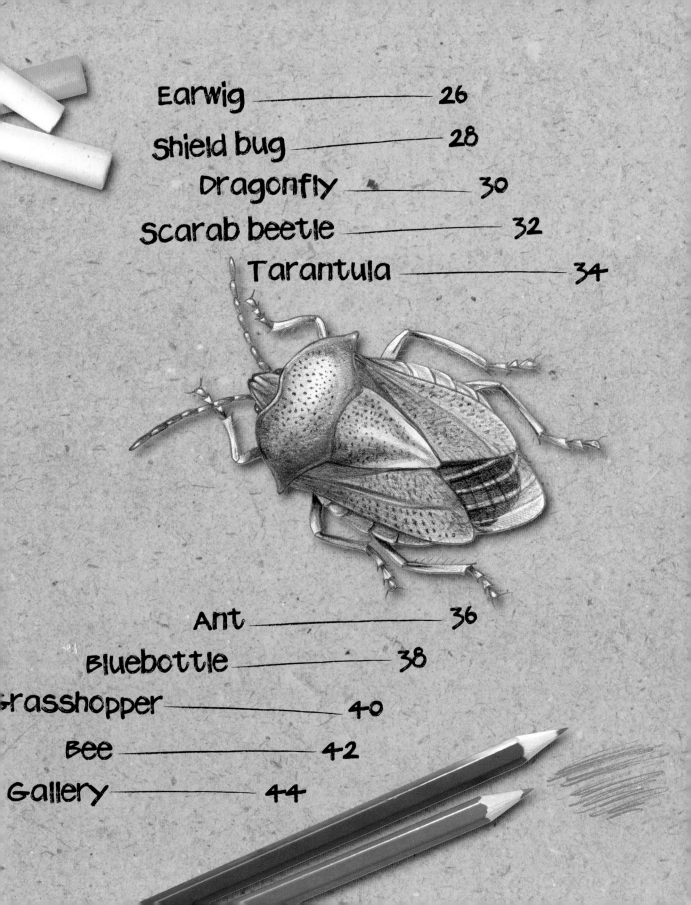

Materials

IT'S EASY TO GET STARTED WHEN YOU WANT TO DRAW BUGS — ALL YOU NEED ARE SOME BASIC ITEMS THAT REALLY DON'T COST MUCH.

Pencils
Use soft pencils (marked with a B) for smudgy lines that are easy to rub out. Hard pencils (marked H) make finer, harsher lines.

Hard pencil

Soft pencil

Coloured pencils
Insects are great fun to draw because they have such a brilliant variety of colour, from muted moths to bright, beautiful beetles. The simplest way to add colour is with coloured pencils, and you can layer them on top of each other to make new colours. Some types can even be blended with water to turn them into watercolours.

Other ways to add colour
Try experimenting with wax crayons, chalk and pastels for different depths and textures.

Paper
Use scraps of paper when you start out — old printer paper is ideal. When you want to produce a finished picture, invest in some art paper.

Try using bumpy or rough paper for instant dramatic texture

Charcoal

Charcoal comes in black, brittle sticks. These are easy to use, and can be smudged and blended to create dramatic pictures full of light and shade.

Felt-tip pens

Some bugs are so boldly coloured that felt tips work well, although it's hard to blend the colours. Use them together with softer lines like pencil and crayon.

Other equipment

Always carry a pad of paper, ready to sketch whenever you see something you like. You'll also need a pencil sharpener, a paintbrush (if you're using watercolour pencils) and erasers. These can be firm, to remove most pencil marks, or soft and kneadable to squash into shape and lift marks off the page, (useful when adding highlights).

Handmade paper and tissue paper can be used for special effects

Anatomy

MOST OF THE BUGS IN THIS BOOK ARE TRUE INSECTS, AND SHARE SIMILAR ANATOMY. OTHER KINDS OF BUG INCLUDE SPIDERS, CENTIPEDES AND SNAILS, AND THEIR BODIES ARE QUITE DIFFERENT.

Insects

Insects are made up of three main parts — head, thorax and abdomen. They have six legs and one or two sets of wings.

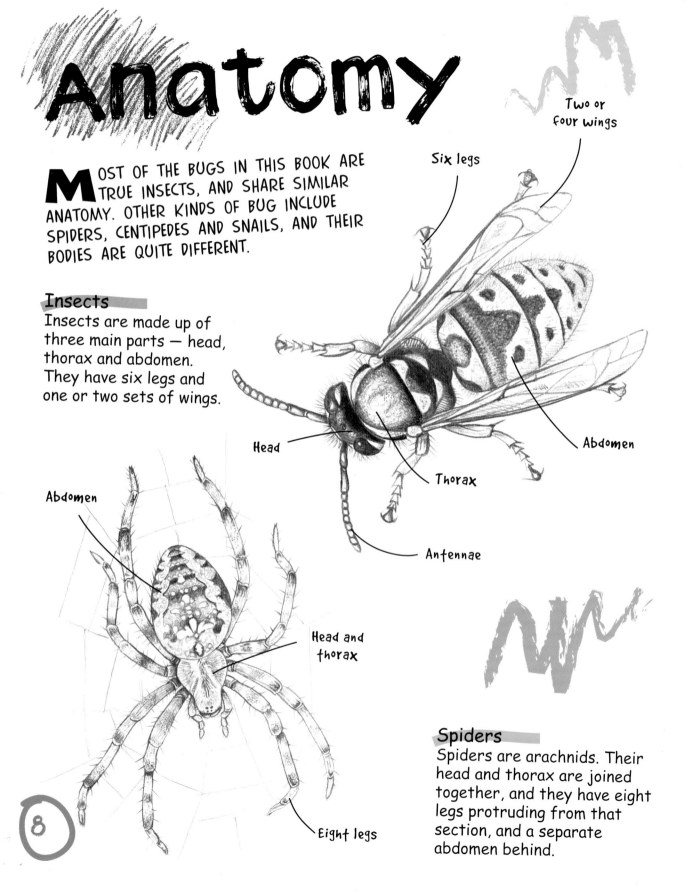

Two or four wings

Six legs

Head

Thorax

Antennae

Abdomen

Abdomen

Head and thorax

Eight legs

Spiders

Spiders are arachnids. Their head and thorax are joined together, and they have eight legs protruding from that section, and a separate abdomen behind.

Snails

Snails are molluscs. Their soft bodies are protected by hard shells, and they have two pairs of tentacles on their heads. Try to find empty snail shells and draw those to start off with — it's a good way to practise shading and perspective.

From above, you can really see the spiral of the snail's shell

Hindwings unfold before flight

Hard forewings hold their shape even when open

Wings

Many insects can fly, and they have a wide variety of wing types and shapes. Beetles have two pairs — hard forewings and delicate hindwings. When the forewings are closed, they fit together to protect the hindwings. Try looking at nature photography to find interesting poses to draw.

Eyes

Bug eyes aren't always visible, but often they are huge, shiny, black orbs. They don't always have two eyes — sometimes it can be many more!

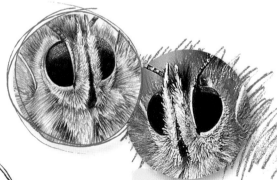

Dragonfly eyes
Shade with lines using a bright colour. Leave some white around the edge.

Butterfly eyes
Use close criss-crossing lines for most of the eye, but make it looser at the top for the highlight.

colour

SOME INSECTS ARE VIVID COLOURS, WHILE OTHERS HAVE MORE SUBTLE SHADES. ALWAYS DRAW WHAT YOU SEE, NOT WHAT YOU THINK YOU KNOW.

Bright

Use photographic reference from books or the internet to get complicated patterns right.

Butterfly patterns are usually symmetrical

Muted

You can be less precise with subtler markings, but vary the tones you use to create interest.

Remember, the shade or colour of the wings might vary on the underside

Iridescence

Some bug colours are iridescent, which means they seem to change as the bug moves. Try blending different colours together on your page, and use paler versions for highlights instead of leaving areas uncoloured.

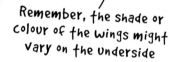

The highlight on this shiny green bug is white and golden yellow

Texture

LOOK CLOSELY AT THE TEXTURE OF WHAT YOU'RE TRYING TO DRAW. IS IT HAIRY OR SMOOTH, ROUGH OR SLIMY? SOME INSECTS HAVE HARD BODY PARTS THAT ARE A MORE SOLID COLOUR. HAIRY ELEMENTS SUCH AS LEGS OR BODIES NEED FEATHERY STROKES.

Hard and smooth
Use contrasting colours on different sections to create the look of a hard, angular bug body.

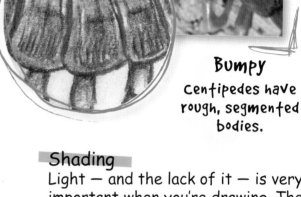

Bumpy
Centipedes have rough, segmented bodies.

Shading
Light — and the lack of it — is very important when you're drawing. The parts that catch the light (most often the upper surfaces) will show more detail than areas in shadow.

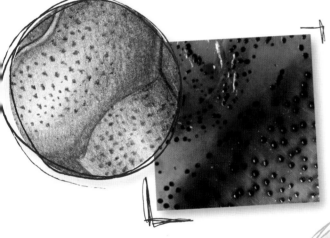

Depth and detail
Use stippling (dots of colour), and hatching (small, parallel lines) for added depth and shadows. For even more emphasis on shadowed areas, use cross-hatching (lines crossing each other). Try different colours for your shadows — mix black with greys, blues, greens, browns and purples.

Hairy
Short, firm pencil strokes will create the appearance of fine hairs.

11

Action

INSECTS MOVE FAST, SO IT'S HARD TO CAPTURE THEM IN MOTION. STUDY PHOTOS TO SEE HOW THEY MOVE. VARY YOUR DRAWINGS BETWEEN 'STILL' SHOTS AND 'ACTION' SHOTS, LIKE A GRASSHOPPER SPRINGING INTO MID-AIR, A DRAGONFLY HOVERING OR A CATERPILLAR INCHING ITS WAY ALONG.

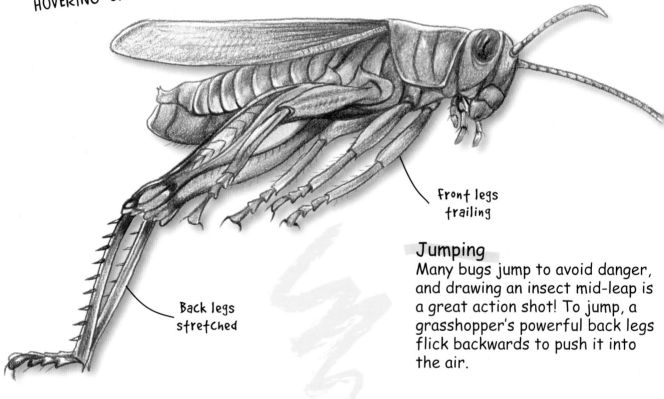

Front legs
trailing

Back legs
stretched

Jumping
Many bugs jump to avoid danger, and drawing an insect mid-leap is a great action shot! To jump, a grasshopper's powerful back legs flick backwards to push it into the air.

Walking
Study how bugs walk. Six-legged bugs will lift one leg on one side and two legs on the opposite side. Legs that are still touching the surface need to touch the shadow, while a space between the shadow and end of the leg suggests it's being lifted and is in the air.

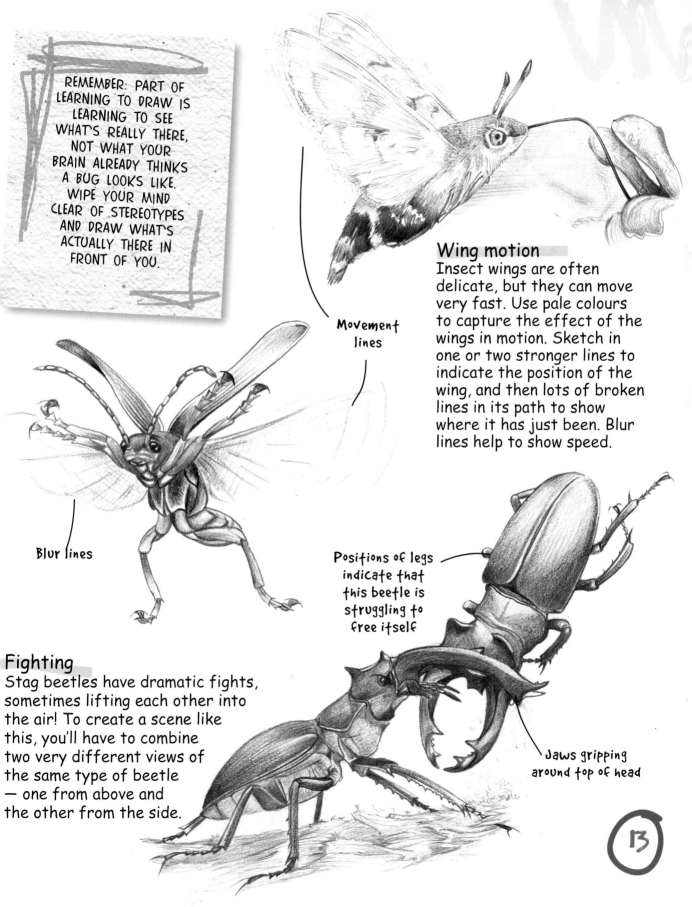

REMEMBER: PART OF LEARNING TO DRAW IS LEARNING TO SEE WHAT'S REALLY THERE, NOT WHAT YOUR BRAIN ALREADY THINKS A BUG LOOKS LIKE. WIPE YOUR MIND CLEAR OF STEREOTYPES AND DRAW WHAT'S ACTUALLY THERE IN FRONT OF YOU.

Movement lines

Wing motion

Insect wings are often delicate, but they can move very fast. Use pale colours to capture the effect of the wings in motion. Sketch in one or two stronger lines to indicate the position of the wing, and then lots of broken lines in its path to show where it has just been. Blur lines help to show speed.

Blur lines

Positions of legs indicate that this beetle is struggling to free itself

Jaws gripping around top of head

Fighting

Stag beetles have dramatic fights, sometimes lifting each other into the air! To create a scene like this, you'll have to combine two very different views of the same type of beetle — one from above and the other from the side.

snail

1 Sketch the basic snail shape – a sausage for the body and a squashed circle for the shell.

Make the sausage fatter at the head end

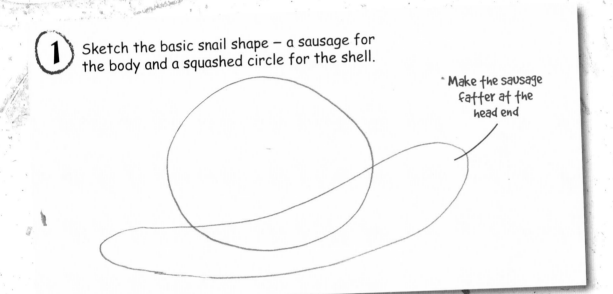

2 Add the basic shapes of the tentacles.

Draw new lines that will add shape to the shell

Slightly reshape the body as shown

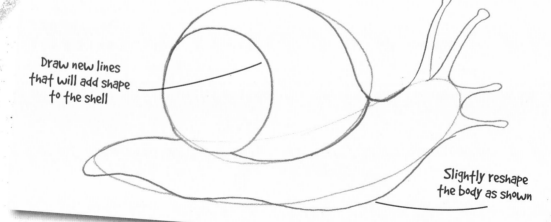

3 Rub out the guidelines and add the swirl on the shell as a solid line. Shade areas of the shell to make it look more three-dimensional.

Add pale lines to the body

The eyes are on the tips of the tentacles

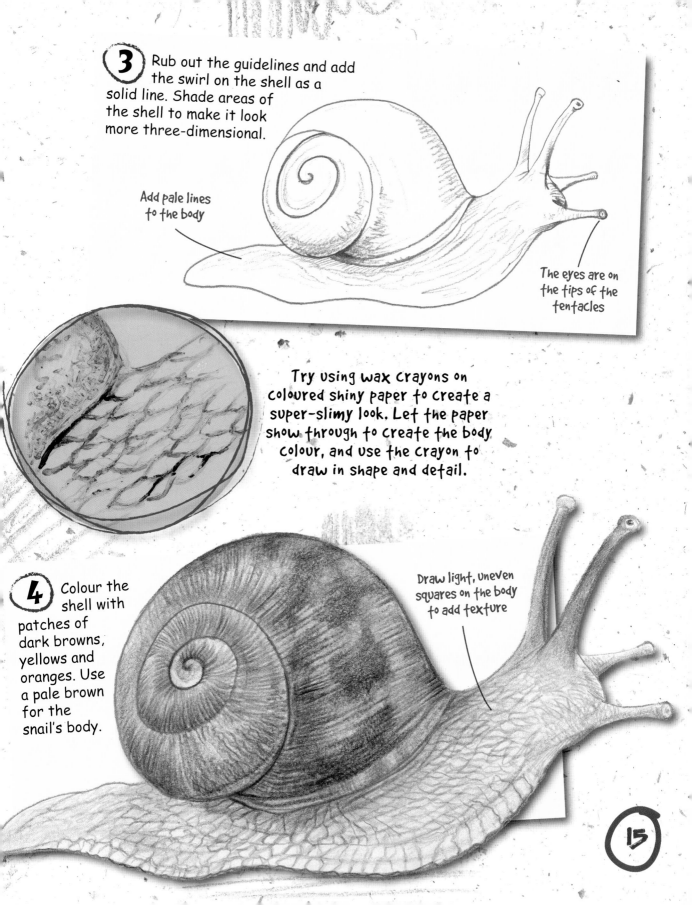

Try using wax crayons on coloured shiny paper to create a super-slimy look. Let the paper show through to create the body colour, and use the crayon to draw in shape and detail.

4 Colour the shell with patches of dark browns, yellows and oranges. Use a pale brown for the snail's body.

Draw light, uneven squares on the body to add texture

Ladybird

1 Draw a large oval and mark a curved line for the wing casings. Add another curved line towards the front to separate the thorax from the body.

The body isn't positioned straight on, so the line for the wings isn't straight down the middle

2 Outline the spots and shape the wing cases. Draw a small curve to mark the position of the head.

Add detail to the thorax

Round off the edges of the wings

3 Draw in detail on the head and add in the antennae.

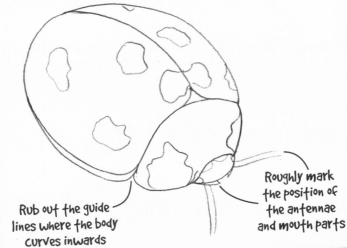

Rub out the guide lines where the body curves inwards

Roughly mark the position of the antennae and mouth parts

4 Draw the legs — not all of them will be visible from this angle. Begin shading the body.

Finish the detail on the legs and antennae

Try drawing on coloured paper. Red paper will create the body colour, so you can just add details and highlights in black and white.

5 Colour the wing cases red, and the head, thorax and legs black. Leave pale highlights to give a shiny finish.

Use hatching in the shaded areas

caterpillar

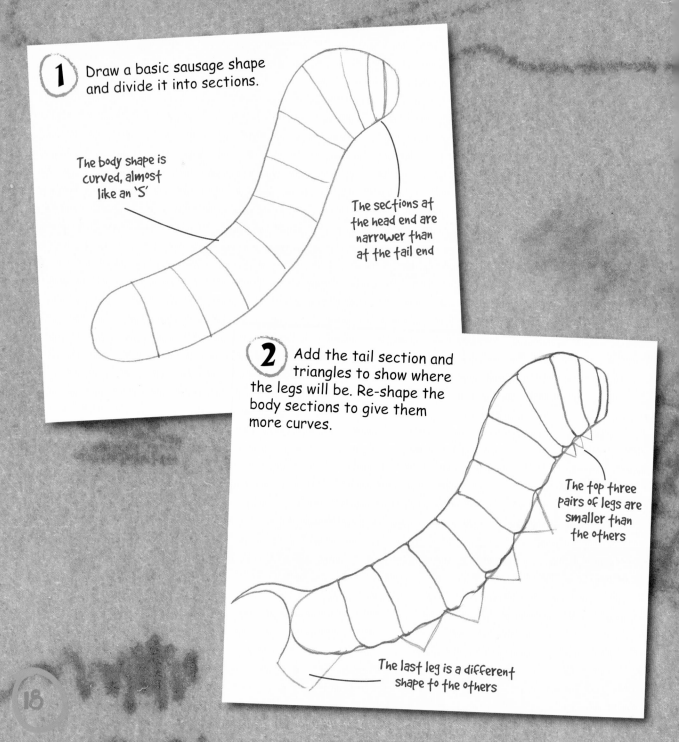

1 Draw a basic sausage shape and divide it into sections.

The body shape is curved, almost like an 'S'

The sections at the head end are narrower than at the tail end

2 Add the tail section and triangles to show where the legs will be. Re-shape the body sections to give them more curves.

The top three pairs of legs are smaller than the others

The last leg is a different shape to the others

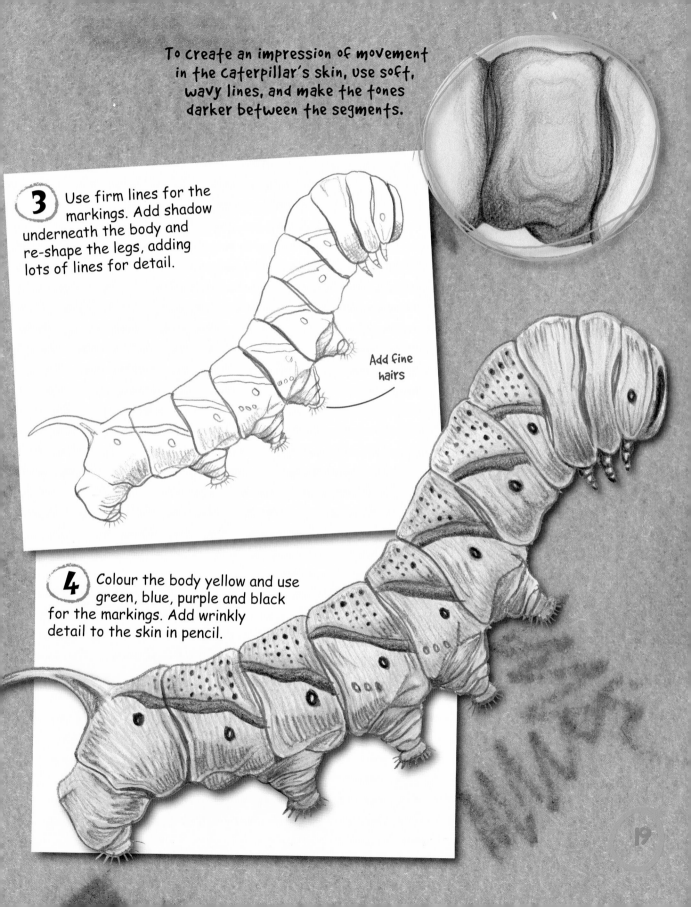

To create an impression of movement in the caterpillar's skin, use soft, wavy lines, and make the tones darker between the segments.

3 Use firm lines for the markings. Add shadow underneath the body and re-shape the legs, adding lots of lines for detail.

Add fine hairs

4 Colour the body yellow and use green, blue, purple and black for the markings. Add wrinkly detail to the skin in pencil.

centipede

1 Draw a long wiggly shape for the body, like a worm.

The sections are narrower where the body bends

Divide the body into sections

2 Add shape to each section, rounding off the corners. Draw in the long antennae.

Each section is overlapped by the one in front of it

The long rear legs are curved and point backwards

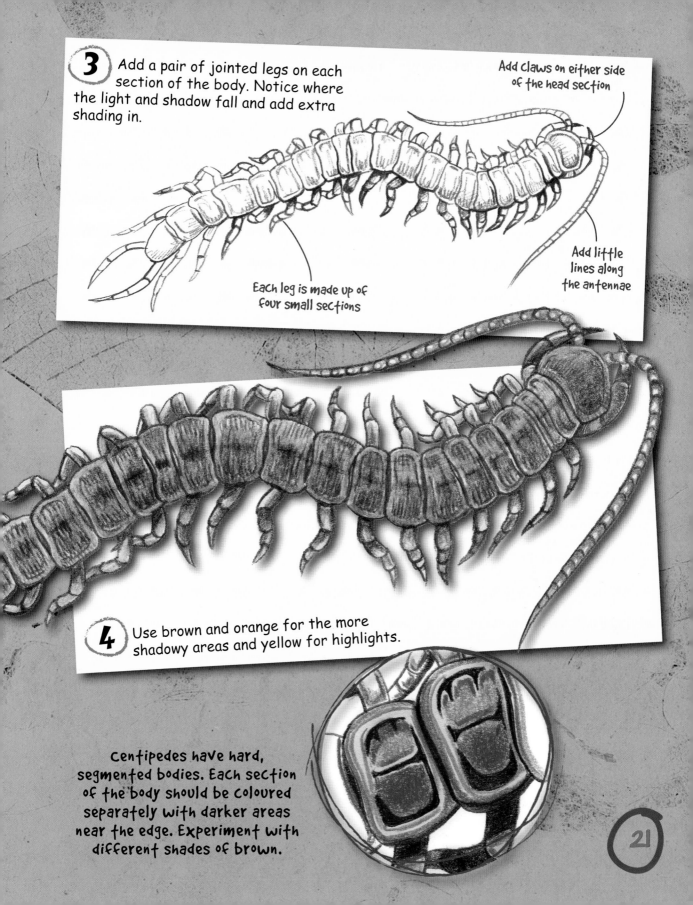

3 Add a pair of jointed legs on each section of the body. Notice where the light and shadow fall and add extra shading in.

Add claws on either side of the head section

Each leg is made up of four small sections

Add little lines along the antennae

4 Use brown and orange for the more shadowy areas and yellow for highlights.

Centipedes have hard, segmented bodies. Each section of the body should be coloured separately with darker areas near the edge. Experiment with different shades of brown.

Butterfly

1 Start with three basic shapes for the butterfly's body and wings, and a circle for the flower head.

Draw the wing shapes overlapping at this stage — eventually the lower wings will cover part of the upper wings

2 Shape the head and mouthparts. Add detail to the wings.

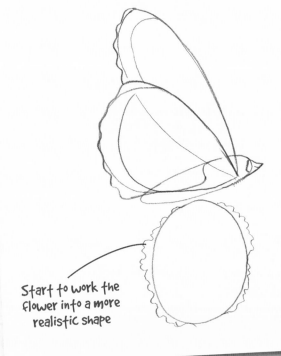

Start to work the flower into a more realistic shape

Butterfly wings are covered in tiny scales. Try using coloured paper as a base, and add dots of darker and lighter shades for detail.

3 Rub out the guidelines and start to mark in the detail of the wing patterns. Add antennae and a curled tongue. Draw six legs resting on the flower.

The butterfly's body is almost furry, so add small lines all around the edge

Draw texture all over the flower, and add the stem

4 Colour the pattern on the wings. Use brown and black to colour the body, and add bright, contrasting colour to the flower.

crane fly

1 Sketch the basic shape: long, thin ovals for the thorax and abdomen, and two wings.

The ovals for the wings have pointed tips

2 Add details to show the head and the sections that make up the abdomen. The head has a bulbous part where the eyes will go, and a pointed mouth piece.

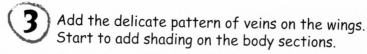

Redraw the ends of the wings where they join the body, making them more slender

3 Add the delicate pattern of veins on the wings. Start to add shading on the body sections.

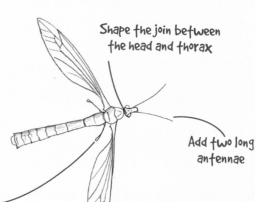

Shape the join between the head and thorax

Add two long antennae

Draw two small, wing-like parts behind the wings

4 Draw in the six long, spindly legs. Each one is made of three main sections with four smaller sections at the ends.

The antennae have tiny feathery lines coming off them

The wings are transparent, so the legs can be drawn in faintly underneath

5 Colour the body pale brown, leaving some white highlights. Add a little pale blue and green to the wings. The eyes are black.

Earwig

1 Start with a long, curved oval for the body divided into sections.

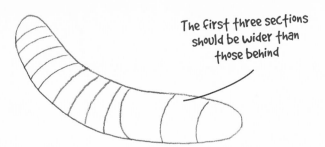

The first three sections should be wider than those behind

2 Add the pointed pincers at the tail end. Give some shape to the body sections.

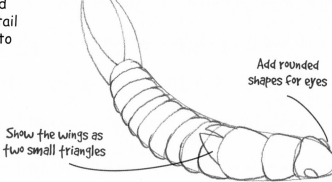

Add rounded shapes for eyes

Show the wings as two small triangles

3 Rub out your guidelines and sketch in the position of the six legs.

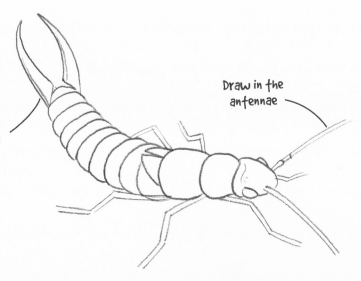

Add definition to the pincers

Draw in the antennae

4 Earwigs are dark-coloured but shiny, so leave pale or uncoloured areas for highlights.

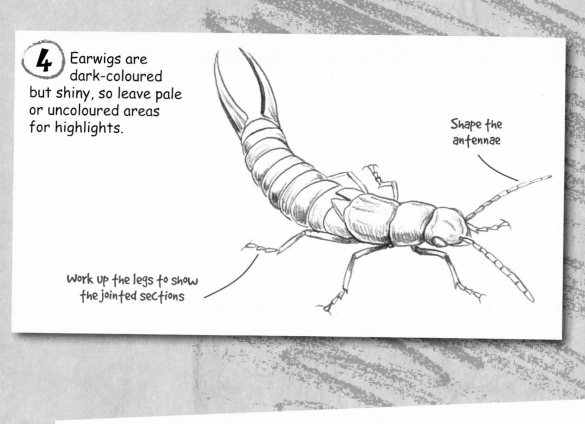

Shape the antennae

Work up the legs to show the jointed sections

5 Colour using shades of brown — darker towards the sides of the body and legs, and lighter on top.

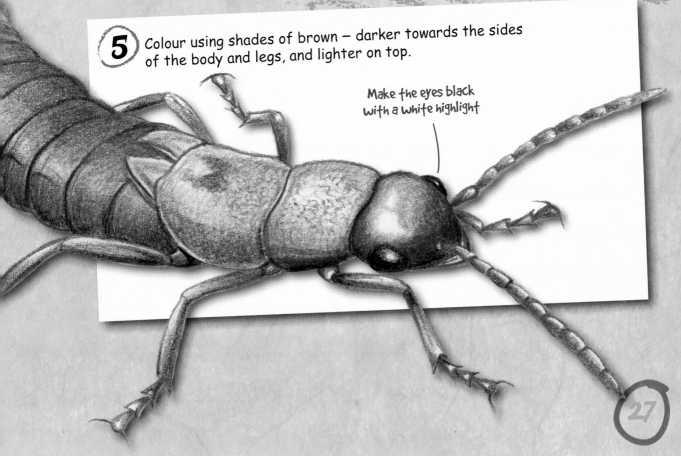

Make the eyes black with a white highlight

shield bug

1 Draw the basic shape – a combination of squares and triangles.

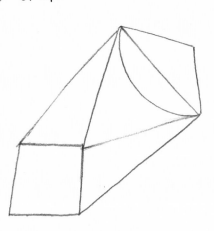

2 Add the head and work over your basic outline to define the body parts.

This hard casing is a curved shape

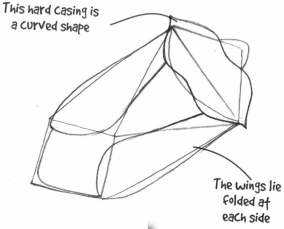

The wings lie folded at each side

3 Roughly sketch in six legs and the antennae. Rub out your guidelines now.

Add the eyes at the sides of the head

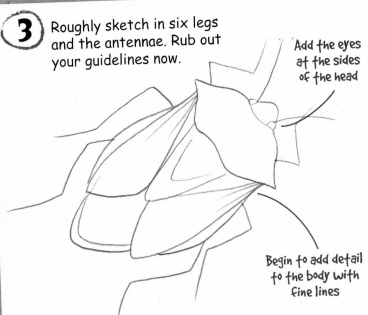

Begin to add detail to the body with fine lines

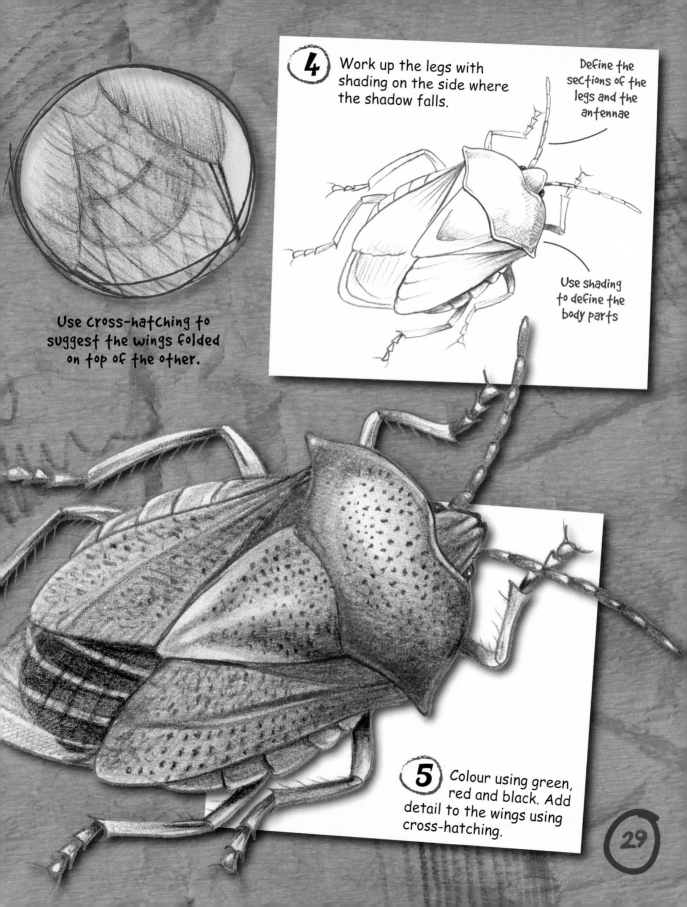

4 Work up the legs with shading on the side where the shadow falls.

Define the sections of the legs and the antennae

Use shading to define the body parts

Use cross-hatching to suggest the wings folded on top of the other.

5 Colour using green, red and black. Add detail to the wings using cross-hatching.

29

Dragonfly

1 Draw a long, thin body and a fatter thorax. Add four wing shapes.

These lower wings should be drawn slightly bigger, because they are closer to us

2 Reshape the front oval to make a separate head and thorax.

Make the body thinner

Add a pointed tail end

3 Sketch in lines for the legs, remembering that not all of them will be visible from this angle. Draw in the large eyes.

Shape the head

Divide the abdomen into sections

Add detail to the wings

Try creating delicate wings by working on paper with flecks of colour in it. Sketch in detail lightly using the point of your pencil.

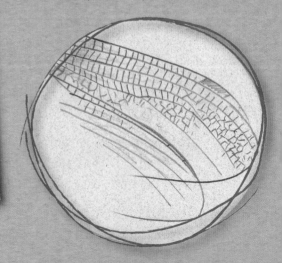

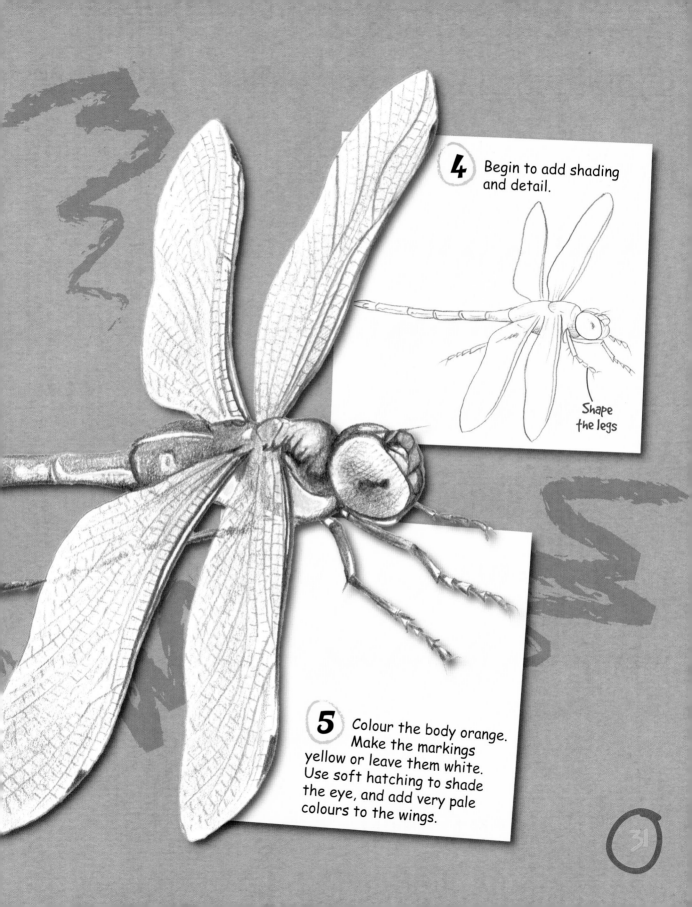

4 Begin to add shading and detail.

Shape the legs

5 Colour the body orange. Make the markings yellow or leave them white. Use soft hatching to shade the eye, and add very pale colours to the wings.

scarab beetle

1 The basic body shape here is simple — overlapping head, thorax and abdomen, all made of circles or ovals.

2 Shape the thorax and add circles for eyes.

Taper the front of the head

Start to sketch in some detail on the hard wing cases

3 Give more definition to the pointed sections at the front of the thorax.

Rework the head to add in more detail

Firm, definite pencil strokes are needed on the wing cases

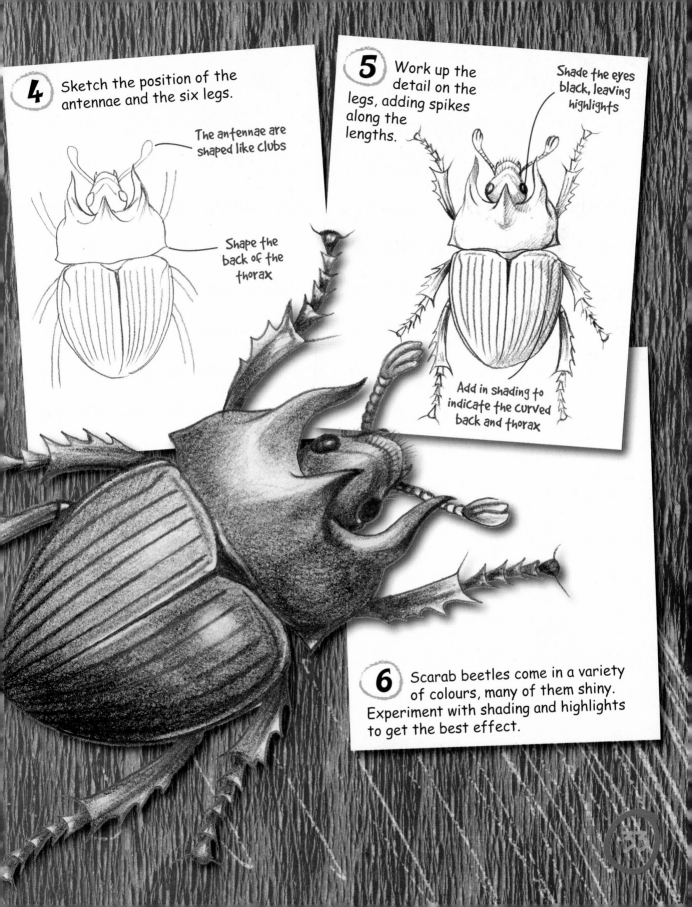

4 Sketch the position of the antennae and the six legs.

The antennae are shaped like clubs

Shape the back of the thorax

5 Work up the detail on the legs, adding spikes along the lengths.

Shade the eyes black, leaving highlights

Add in shading to indicate the curved back and thorax

6 Scarab beetles come in a variety of colours, many of them shiny. Experiment with shading and highlights to get the best effect.

Tarantula

1 Use two ovals for the basic body shape. Add an outer rim to the front oval and mark the position of all eight legs coming off this section.

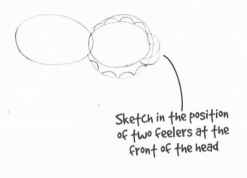

Sketch in the position of two feelers at the front of the head

2 Draw the first sections of each of the eight legs and the two front feelers.

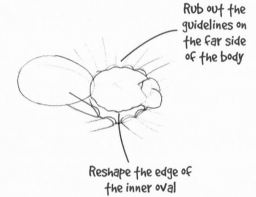

Rub out the guidelines on the far side of the body

Reshape the edge of the inner oval

3 Continue sketching in the legs and feelers, drawing each one in small sections.

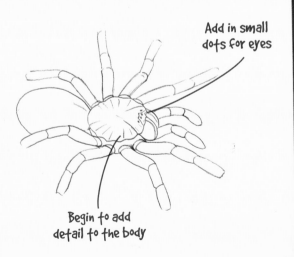

Add in small dots for eyes

Begin to add detail to the body

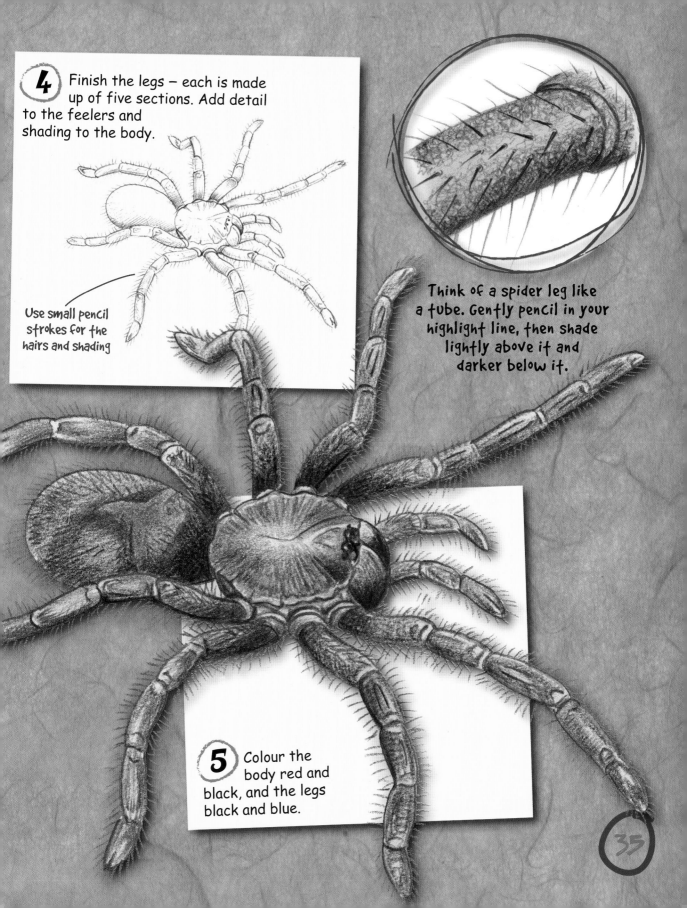

4 Finish the legs — each is made up of five sections. Add detail to the feelers and shading to the body.

Use small pencil strokes for the hairs and shading

Think of a spider leg like a tube. Gently pencil in your highlight line, then shade lightly above it and darker below it.

5 Colour the body red and black, and the legs black and blue.

35

Ant

1 Draw a faint body line to position the ovals for the head, thorax and abdomen.

Join the body parts with a small circle to get the spacing right for later

Mark where the eye will be with an oval

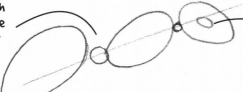

2 Reshape the abdomen so it has a point at the rear end.

Add the ant's jaws, shaped like a beak

3 Draw in the sections of the thorax and abdomen. Sketch in the legs.

Lightly pencil in the antennae

The whole of each leg is visible on this side of the body

Add a line for the twig it is standing on

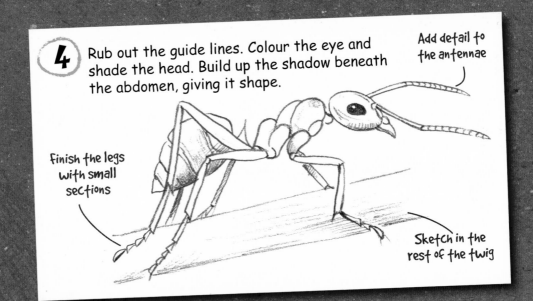

4 Rub out the guide lines. Colour the eye and shade the head. Build up the shadow beneath the abdomen, giving it shape.

Add detail to the antennae

Finish the legs with small sections

Sketch in the rest of the twig

5 Colour a rich brown, leaving shiny white highlights along the back and around the joints.

Bluebottle

1 Start your picture with the basic shapes of the head, body and wings.

The wing shapes aren't positioned symmetrically

The head is a small oval

2 Divide the body into five evenly spaced sections.

Use an egg-shape to outline the position of the thorax

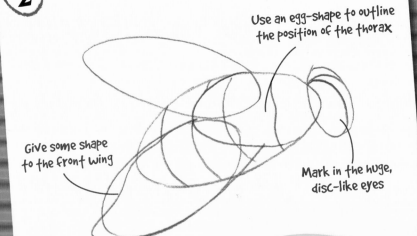

Give some shape to the front wing

Mark in the huge, disc-like eyes

Bluebottles have a metallic sheen, which is hard to recreate on paper. Try leaving white highlights, then shading around them in blue, purple and finally, black.

3 Add detail to the head. Use cross-hatching on the visible eye, and draw in the mouthparts.

Add in small hairs

The egg-shaped thorax crosses the abdomen

Start to add more detail to the wings

4 Draw the legs — only five are visible from this angle.

Add lines of texture to the wings

Use angled hatch lines on the abdomen

5 Colour in blues and greys. Make the thorax pale and the abdomen darker towards the rear. Colour the details on the head brown.

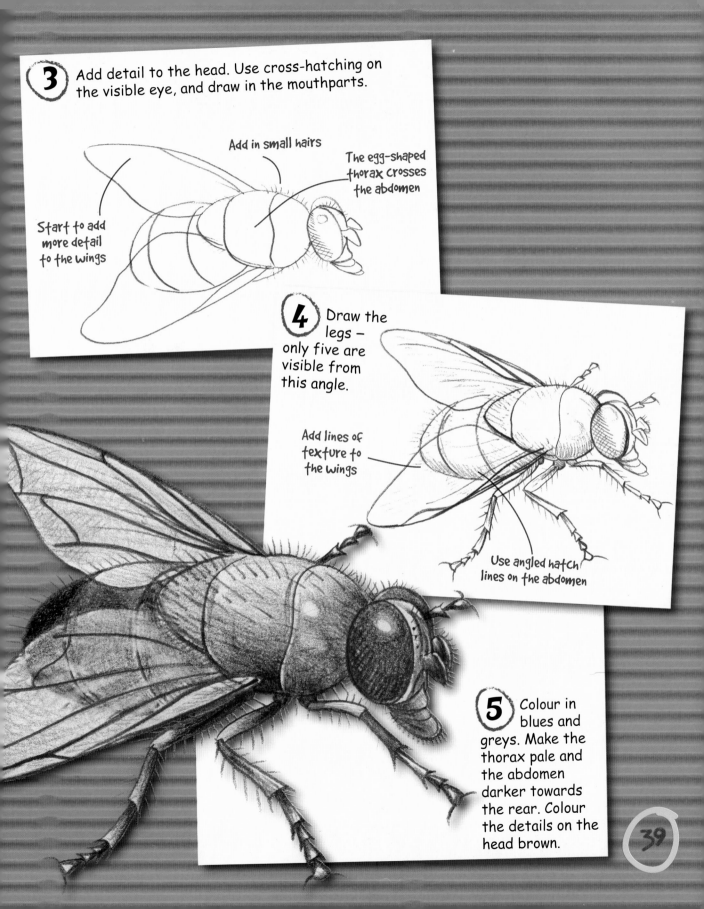

Grasshopper

1 Start with a basic triangular body shape divided into three sections.

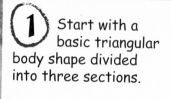

Draw an oval to mark the position of the eye

Extend these lines for the antennae

2 Carefully draw in the shape and detail of the thorax and wings. Fill out the antennae.

Redraw the thorax and head to round off the sharp corners

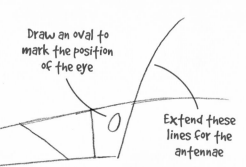

The abdomen is divided into evenly-spaced sections

3 Rub out the guidelines. Add the basic leg shapes, drawing over the body where necessary.

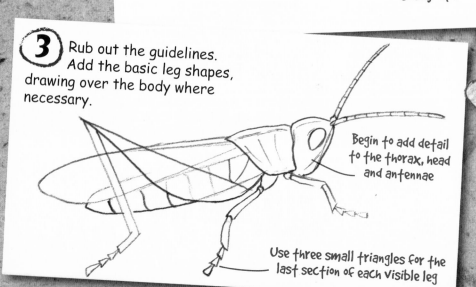

Begin to add detail to the thorax, head and antennae

Use three small triangles for the last section of each visible leg

4 Work up the detail on the legs, changing the outline and adding markings as shown.

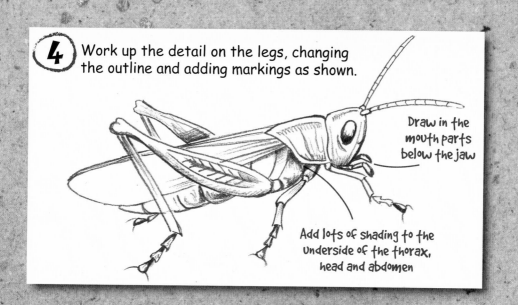

Draw in the mouth parts below the jaw

Add lots of shading to the underside of the thorax, head and abdomen

5 Colour using green, brown and orange, using darker shades where body parts overlap and cast shadows.

Bee

1 Study the pictures carefully before you start to draw the basic overlapping shapes.

These two ovals make up the abdomen and thorax

These two ovals make up the head

2 Divide the body into sections for the stripes and overall shape.

The wings sit on top of the thorax

The faint dividing line will help you position the antennae

Draw in crescent shapes for the eyes

3 Sketch the position of the antennae and visible legs.

Give the wings more shape

Add detail to the head and draw the jaws

Use tiny scribbled lines to give the body texture

4 Finish shaping the legs and antennae. Add more detail to the wings and body.

Make eyes look rounded and shiny by shading most of it closely, but hatching a vertical strip to create a highlight.

5 Use lines of colour for the veins on the wings. The body needs defined dark stripes and a mixture of yellow and darker orange.

Use blue and black to colour darker areas

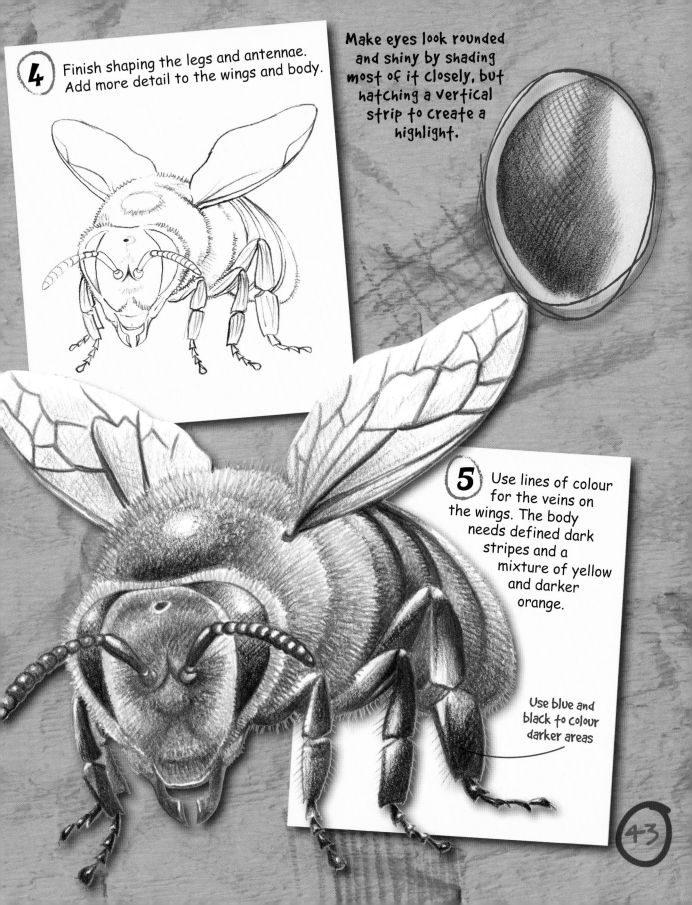

Gallery

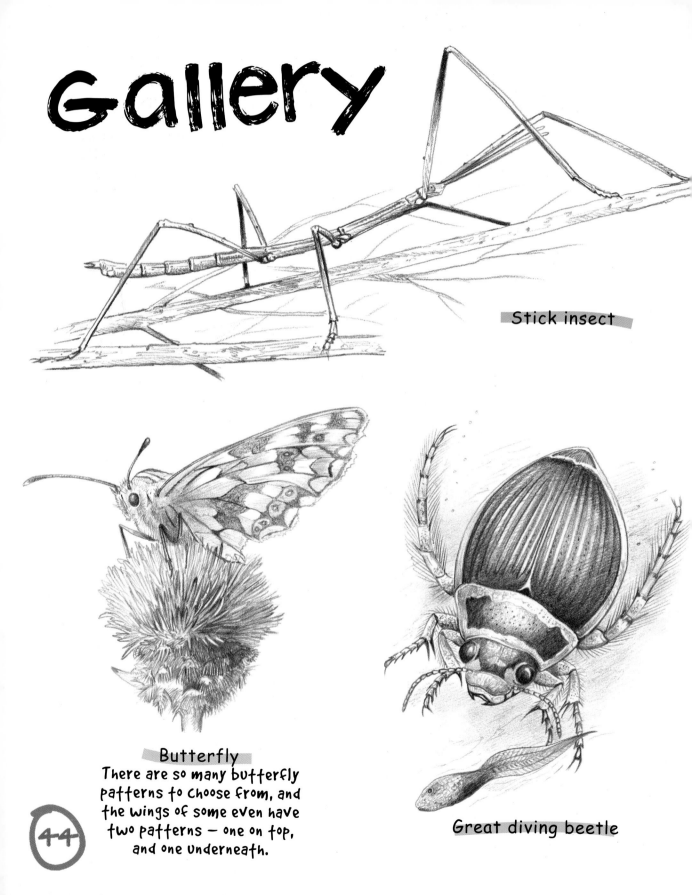

Stick insect

Butterfly
There are so many butterfly patterns to choose from, and the wings of some even have two patterns — one on top, and one underneath.

Great diving beetle

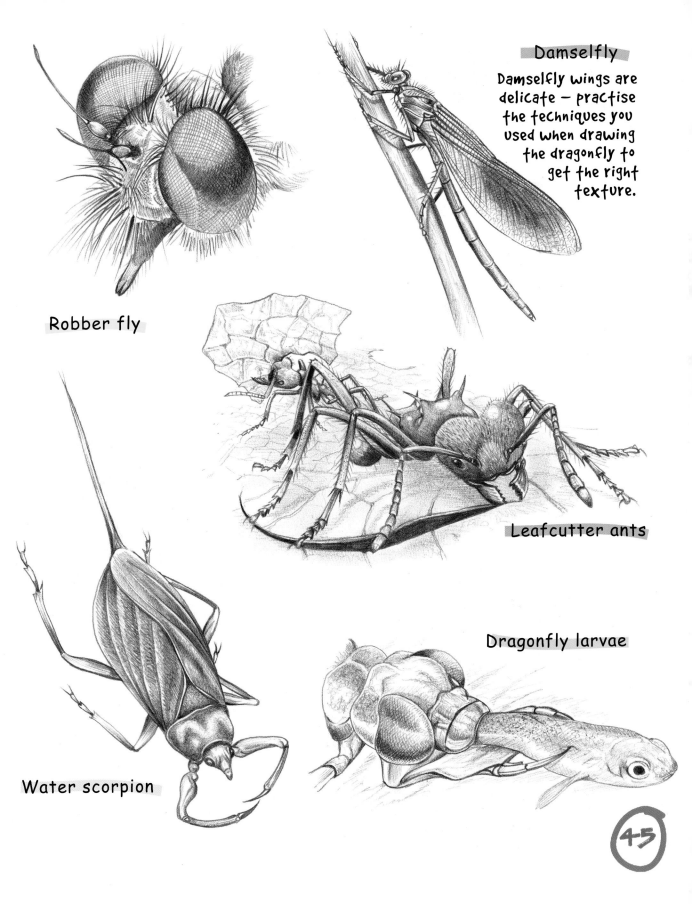

Robber fly

Damselfly wings are delicate — practise the techniques you used when drawing the dragonfly to get the right texture.

Leafcutter ants

Dragonfly larvae

Water scorpion

4-5

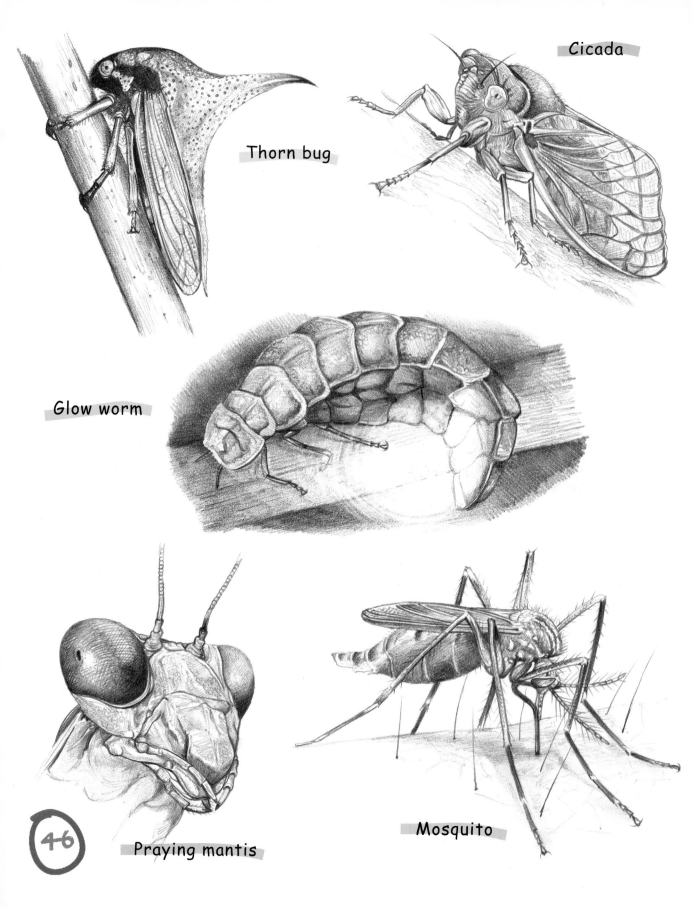

Thorn bug

Cicada

Glow worm

Praying mantis

Mosquito

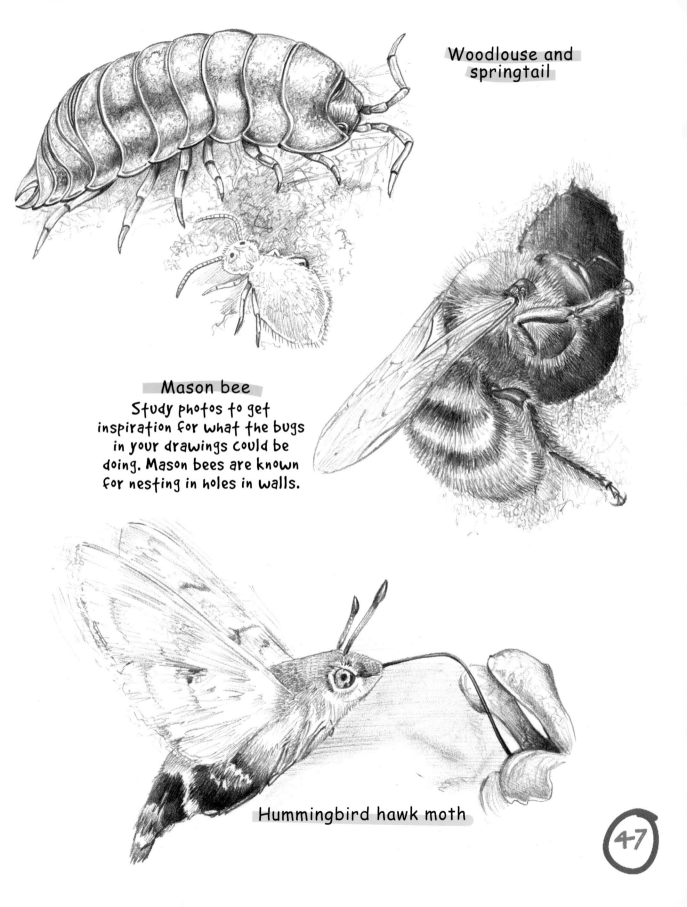

Woodlouse and springtail

Mason bee
Study photos to get inspiration for what the bugs in your drawings could be doing. Mason bees are known for nesting in holes in walls.

Hummingbird hawk moth

First published in 2008 by Miles Kelly Publishing Ltd
Harding's Barn, Bardfield End Green, Thaxted, Essex, CM6 3PX, UK

Copyright © Miles Kelly Publishing Ltd 2008

This edition published 2015

2 4 6 8 10 9 7 5 3

PUBLISHING DIRECTOR Belinda Gallagher
CREATIVE DIRECTOR Jo Cowan
EDITORIAL DIRECTOR Rosie Neave
DESIGNERS Jo Cowan, Kayleigh Allen
REPROGRAPHICS Stephan Davis, Thom Allaway, Anthony Cambray
PRODUCTION Elizabeth Collins, Caroline Kelly

ISBN 978-1-78209-912-3

Printed in China

British Library Cataloguing-in-Publication Data
A catalogue record for this book is available from the British Library

ACKNOWLEDGEMENTS
The publishers would like to thank the following sources
for the use of their photographs:
Cover pencils Yuri Samsonov/Shutterstock.com
Page 6 pencils StudioAraminta/Fotolia.com; 7 Feng Yu/Fotolia.com,
quayside/Fotolia.com, Stephanie Connell/Fotolia.com; 10 Copyright:
Ruta Saulyte-Laurinaviciene/Shutterstock.com; 11 shocky/Fotolia.com;
20–21 deardone/Fotolia.com; 22–23 deardone/Fotolia.com

All other photographs are from:
digitalSTOCK, digitalvision, Dreamstime.com,
ImageState, iStockphoto.com, John Foxx, PhotoAlto,
PhotoDisc, PhotoEssentials, PhotoPro, Stockbyte

Made with paper from a sustainable forest

www.mileskelly.net
info@mileskelly.net